O Blessed Trinity,
a Heaven on earth for Thee
my heart through love would be!

Living with GOD in My Heart

A Meditation

Simple reflections on a very beautiful, consoling, sanctifying and amazing, yet oft-forgotten grace given to us in Baptism.

+A. A. Noser, S.V.D.

ST. PAUL EDITIONS

First printing 1932
Fifteen printings
141,000 copies

Revised edition 1979

Library of Congress Cataloging in Publication Data
Noser, A. A.
    Living with God in my heart.

    1. Meditations. I. Title.
BX2182.2.N666   1980   248.4   80-27015

ISBN 0-8198-4403-9 cloth
ISBN 0-8198-4404-7 paper

Printed in U.S.A. by the Daughters of St. Paul
50 St. Paul's Ave., Boston, MA 02130

The Daughters of St. Paul are an international congregation
of religious women serving the Church with the communications
media.

Immaculate Spouse of the Holy Spirit—
Heart of Mary, Holy Temple of God
The original of this picture forms the centerpiece of the
beautiful altar of the Blessed Virgin Mary in Holy Spirit
Church at St. Gabriel's Foreign Mission Seminary, S.V.D., at
Moedling, Austria.

CONTENTS

Foreword

The heart of every human being is hungry, hungry for love, hungry for happiness, hungry for deep peace, the fruit of satisfied love. In their search, many follow false lights, false paths—riches, honor, power, pleasure, sex, drugs, drink—but the more they drink from these deceitful waters, the greater their thirst becomes. Others seek nobler and higher sources—learning, science, travel, social work, service of their fellowmen, etc. Still others show their contempt for earthly comforts and pleasures and seek to satisfy their hearts' craving by various forms of religion. We call to mind the Jesus People, Children of God, hippies, Moonies, TM, and other forms of Oriental mysticism. But none of them bring full and lasting satisfaction. Happiness cannot permanently be found in following a system, an ideal, a cause, a creed, a code or something similar, for these are all impersonal, and the human heart craves a person to satisfy its hunger fully and permanently.

Many saints followed these paths in their earlier years, only to find them vain and empty, and in the end their search ended in God. St. Francis of Assisi is an outstanding example. But perhaps more than any other, the renowned St. Augustine tried all these roads, but in vain. Having at last found what he had been seeking for years, he gave expression to his joy in those immortal words: "You have made us for Yourself, O Lord, and our heart is restless until it rests in You!" God, the Infinitely Lovable, the Highest Good —He alone is the only answer to this hunger of the human heart, the final goal of man's restless search.

But once found, God not only fully satisfies this hunger, but leads us to the highest heights of holiness, for He said to Abraham: "Walk before me (live in my presence) and be perfect (you will be happy and holy)."

I
GOD

Who Is God? What Is God?

For many people God is just a little three-lettered word: g-o-d. For others He is a mysterious, impersonal, but very real powerful force, blind yet strong, like a cyclone, a waterfall or the power of gravity. This power is something very real, very true, so mighty that it cannot be resisted, terrible and frightening, just because it is blind and impersonal. For others God is indeed a personal being, an all-seeing eye that searches the very depths of mind and heart and whom not the least thing escapes—someone to be feared greatly, never to be offended, lest there be quick and heavy punishment.

Such ideas of God can never satisfy the hunger of man's heart, can never encourage intimate relations between God and ourselves. Rather, they fill the heart with the dread that causes people to tremble at the mysterious power of the magic of the sorcerer.

Our Ideas about God

Human language can never express what God really is, for as long as we are in this world the human mind cannot conceive Him as He is. In theology we say that all our ideas about God are analogous, that is, there is some slight similarity between our ideas and the divine Reality. Thus we say that men are good, kind, compassionate, merciful, beautiful, etc., but when we say these things and think of the best of men and then multiply them many times over to apply them to God, we are still far from seeing what God is. It is like comparing the chirping of a sparrow with the great masterpieces of Mozart or Bach: there is only one thing in which they are similar—both are sounds —but there the similarity ends. It is like comparing the light and heat of a candle, or even a spark, with that of the sun. There is similarity, but how insignificant! So it is when we apply our ideas to God: He is infinitely exalted above all of them.

But this God, who stands so far above by reason of His infinite perfections, has chosen to stand in the most intimate relation to us: He is really and truly our Father; we are in very truth His dear children, whom He loves with a love far beyond our power to understand. But of this we shall say more later.

God Is a Person

God then is not some*thing,* but someONE, a Person. All our ideas are taken from the things around us, the visible world, and so our idea of a person is taken from that of a human person. A human person is an individual being, independent from all others, having intelligence and free will, and united to a body and a soul. It is this person which makes our human nature—our body and soul—independent, individual, responsible. We apply this very limited and imperfect idea to God to try to understand Him. But the differences are far greater than the similarities: human ideas can never express the divine, the infinite. For this we must wait for heaven, where we shall be given the special help needed to see God as He really is. The first second of this amazing bliss will never pass, but will last forever. For eternal bliss consists in seeing, loving, possessing and enjoying God. Once ours, it can never be lost.

But God, who is so far above our power of understanding Him, has given us a special knowledge of Himself even here on earth by revelation.

Three Persons, One God

God has told us that He is indeed only one God, one divine Nature, but He has also told us some of the deepest secrets of His inner life. He has told us that there are three Persons in this one God and that each of them possesses fully the one divine Nature. This He has told us through His Son, who as Second Person in God replaced a human person in a true human nature given to Him by the ever Blessed Virgin Mary, so that He was fully God and fully man.

The Father takes His origin from no one, and from all eternity the Son is born of the Father, and the Holy Spirit is breathed forth by both as divine Love. All three are equal in everything: each is eternal, all-knowing, almighty. God exists in a changeless present: with Him there was no before and there is no after or future; there is not even a present as we understand it, for our present is passing, merely a split second between past and future, before and after. With God it is, so to say, a split second which stands still and includes all that we call before and after. In God everything IS: the Son *is* born of the Father and the Holy Spirit *is* breathed forth by both, for this belongs essentially to the inner life of God, and we shall see it in heaven. On earth we know it by Faith only because it has pleased God to reveal it to us.

In the *Creed of the People of God,* we pray: "We believe in the Father who eternally begets the Son; in the Son, the Word of God, who is eternally begotten; in the Holy Spirit, the uncreated Person who proceeds from the Father and the Son as their eternal love" (Pope Paul VI).

God—Supremely Lovable in Himself

What we can know about God makes it clear that He is the highest, the supreme, the most lovable Good —all that the heart of man hungers for. The First Vatican Council speaking of God says: "There is one living and true God, who is almighty, eternal, everywhere present, far beyond our power to understand, limitless in mind and will and every desirable good quality. In Himself and of Himself He is happy without limits, and no created being can tell how highly He is exalted above everything which actually exists outside of Himself or of which we can form an idea."

God possesses not only every existing good quality or perfection which we know, but also millions of others of which we do not know, and each one is without limits. These good qualities in God are so many that no creature is able to count them, and each of them is without limits. They are like an immense ocean without bottom or shores. Since these good qualities are without number and without limits, they cannot be increased or decreased. God has every kind of goodness and beauty which we see in creatures but in an infinitely more exalted measure.

As was mentioned above, our knowledge of these good qualities as they are in God is as feeble as the light of a candle or even a tiny spark beside the sun. How great and lovable God is for His own sake, because of what He is!

God Loves Us

God who is infinitely and eternally happy in Himself does not need anything outside of Himself to add to His happiness. But Goodness by its very nature feels the need of pouring itself out, of sharing its joys with others, of making others happy. To do this God brought many kinds of beings into existence by His wisdom and power. The First Vatican Council speaking of this says: "Out of His Goodness and by His Almighty Power, not to make Himself happy or to add to His happiness, but to show His perfections (good qualities) through the good things He would give to His creatures, God made out of nothing the spiritual and material world. By His Providence He watches over and guides all things to their goal, mightily and sweetly arranging everything." God made all these things for us, for mankind. But let us look at things a bit more closely.

God the Creator

We see God's wisdom and power in the things around us: the vast extent of the skies, the immensity, size and number of the stars in space which seems endless. Many of these are so far away that even with the most powerful modern instruments we have not been able to catch sight of them. But this wisdom and power is seen also in the little things that God has made. We think of the countless kinds of plants—each one, no matter how small its seed, choosing from the same piece of ground what it needs to form its own kind of root, stem, leaves, flowers of many shapes and colors, and the great variety of fruits. We think of the many kinds of insects, birds, fish and other things, the mountains and rivers, the vast oceans. Yes, even the tiny things that can be seen only through a powerful microscope. We know that no man is so wise and powerful that he can think of, much less make all these things. Only Someone with limitless wisdom and power can do this—He is God.

But God is more than just the sum total of all these things we see and can think of, for He could go on creating ever more and more, ever greater and greater worlds and still not come to the end of His wisdom and power. All that we see, know, and ever can know about God is only a single ray of a feeble flashlight compared with the sun. He and He alone is infinitely lovable and can satisfy the hunger of the human heart.

God's Still Greater Love

God made all these things not for themselves, but for a greater creature which was to follow. When all was ready, He made the king and ruler of this vast universe—He made man. He breathed His divine life into him, made him His child and was most eager to have him share in His own boundless and eternal happiness. But man spoiled God's plan by disobedience. Still God did not reject him. He made a new and even more wonderful plan—one which in even our wildest dreams we could never have imagined—to bring man to the happiness He had prepared for him. He went, so to speak, to the very limit of even divine wisdom and power and love to show how eager He was to have man be eternally happy. He sent His one and only Son, the Second Person of the Blessed Trinity, to become a member of the human race, to bring man back to God, by having this beloved Son endure the most shameful and painful death on a cross, in order that man might realize the immensity and intensity of His love and His eagerness for man's happiness. He has given back to us the divine life, made us His children again, members of His Church and through her given us this very Savior as food and drink to nourish us as children of God. He guides and guards us through all the trials and temptations of life. This is clearly stated by St. John: "God loved the world so much that he gave his only-begotten Son for its salvation" (John 3:16).

Again: "God's love for us is revealed in this, that God sent his only Son into the world so that we could have life through him" (1 John 3:9). And in amazement he exclaims: "Behold what love the Father has for us by letting us be called God's children; and that is what we really are. But it has not yet appeared what we shall be" (1 John 3:1). The same thought is expressed again and again by St. Paul.

God Is Love

God not only loves us, but "God *is* Love" (1 John 4:9). He is all eagerness to make us happy with Himself, to share His bliss with Him in heaven forever. We can never repeat this enough: Our hunger for happiness is as nothing when compared with the eagerness which God has for making us happy. This eagerness of God is personal; it is for each of us individually. Each of us can say with St. Paul: "Christ has loved *me* and delivered himself up for *me*." It is a great joy to believe this and to believe it without a shadow of doubt, without a speck of suspicion. God loves and cares for me as if I were the only one on whom He lavished His attention. I am not just one of a crowd. The sun pours down an abundance of its light and heat on the whole of creation, but even the tiniest blade of grass gets all the sunshine which it needs for its growth.

God, our Father, cares and provides for the birds, clothes the wild flowers with a beauty all their own, even numbers the hairs of my head, as our Lord assures us—even the things too insignificant for us to care about are a part of His concern for us. Yes, God, our Father, loves each of us immensely more than we can imagine. His one great desire is to satisfy this hunger of our hearts for love and happiness, for He Himself has put it into our hearts, and He alone can satisfy it.

But alas! God is so far away! We want those whom we love to be near to us, to be present, we want to be with them often, to speak familiarly with them, to enjoy their love and their presence. But God is in heaven—so far away! True, God is in heaven, where He removes the veil and shows Himself in His infinite beauty to the saints there, but He is also very near to us, closer than we are to ourselves, more intimately than we can understand. Let us look into this a bit more deeply.

II
GOD'S
SPECIAL PRESENCE
IN MY HEART

The Fact

Yes, God is in heaven. But heaven seems so far away! God is everywhere also. But someone who is everywhere seems almost the same as one who is nowhere. We who rely in everything on sense-knowledge cannot picture such a being as real, let alone live intimately with Him.

But God's love for us is so great that He comes to our hearts, to each one of us personally, individually, if we sincerely desire to have Him. He tells us this in many places in the New Testament—too many for us to quote here.

Our Lord's Words

Our Lord said: "If anyone loves me, my Father will love him and we will both come and make our abode with him" (John 14:14). But more often He speaks of the Holy Spirit, who is the Spirit of Truth and Love, as the One who is sent as the Father's gift to us: "I will ask the Father and he will give you another Helper, the Spirit of Truth, to be with you forever. He will be with you and in you" (John 15:16). "If I go I shall send the Helper to you" (John 16:7). "From his breast shall flow a fountain of living water." This Jesus said of the Spirit that those were to receive who believed in Him (John 7:37-38). "The Spirit of the Father will be speaking in you" (Mt. 10:19).

St. Paul

St. Paul calls attention of his converts to this truth many times in his letters. Only a few examples will be given here. "Do you not know that your members (of the body) are the temple of the Holy Spirit who is in you, whom you have received from God, and you are not your own? Glorify and bear God in your bodies" (1 Corinthians 6:19-20). "We are the temple of the Living God, as God says, 'I will live in them'" (2 Corinthians 6:16). "The love of God has been diffused in our hearts by the Holy Spirit who is given to us" (Romans 5:5). "The Spirit you have received is the Spirit of sons and makes you cry out 'Abba! Father!'" (Romans 8:15) "God himself has anointed us, marking us with his seal, and giving us the pledge, the Holy Spirit, that we carry in our heart" (2 Corinthians 1:22). "The Spirit of God has made his home in you" (Romans 8:9). "You have been stamped with the seal of the Holy Spirit of Promise, the pledge of our inheritance" (Ephesians 1:14). "If the Spirit of him who raised Jesus from the dead is living in you...he will give life to your mortal bodies through his Spirit living in you" (Romans 8:11).

Evidently, for St. Paul this truth was very important for his Christians and was intended to play a great part in their daily lives. Otherwise, why this strong and repeated insistence on it by him?

St. John

A few texts from St. John: "Whoever confesses that Jesus is the Son of God, God abides in him and he in God. God is Love and he who abides in love abides in God and God in him" (1 John 4:15). "Whoever keeps God's commandments lives in God and God in him. By this we know that he lives in us by the Spirit that he has given to us" (1 John 3:24). "Behold, I stand at the door and knock. If anyone opens to me, I will come in and share his meal with him and he with me" (Apocalypse 3:20).

The Holy Spirit

As is seen, many of these texts speak of the Holy Spirit living in our heart, and for this reason this presence is often called "the Indwelling of the Holy Spirit." But the Father and the Son are also present. This way of speaking—"attributing" this presence to the Holy Spirit, as theologians say—is used because this presence is a work of love and in the Blessed Trinity the Holy Spirit is the Spirit of Love and all works of love are ascribed to Him. Hence it is said that the Holy Spirit is sent as the Father's gift to the soul, but in reality the soul in sanctifying grace is the home of all three Persons of the most blessed Trinity, Father, Son and Holy Spirit. But to continue!

The Fathers of the Church

That these passages from Holy Scripture were understood literally from the earliest days of the Church is clear from the sermons of the Fathers of the Church and from their writings. Thus St. Ignatius of Antioch, bishop and martyr, wrote to the Ephesians: "You are all bearers of God, bearers of His temple, bearers of Christ." When he was treated with contempt by the Roman Emperor Trajan for being a Christian, he boldly replied: "Let no one treat with contempt Theophorus (God-bearer), for I bear God within me."

Tertullian encourages the martyrs in prison with the words: "Grieve not the Holy Spirit who has entered the prison with you, for if he had not gone with you, you would not be there. Endeavor to keep Him that He may lead you thence to the Lord."

Origen wrote: "I know that my soul is a dwelling-place. Of whom? Of God, of Christ, of the Holy Spirit."

St. Cyril of Alexandria writes: "Those are heaven in whom God dwells and whom He accompanies."

Pope St. Gregory the Great: "Since God is Wisdom, and the soul of the just is the seat of Wisdom, while heaven is called the seat of God, it follows that the soul of the just is heaven."

Finally, we have the beautiful testimony of St. Augustine: "Too late have I come to love You, O Beauty so ancient, yet so new. Too late have I come to love You. And see You were within me, and I without."

The Saints

Since St. Leonidas (martyred in 204) could not attend services with the Christians because of the persecutions, he would bend reverently over the cradle of his infant son and kiss his breast, explaining to those who asked the reason: "I adore God present in the body of my infant son who since Baptism is a temple of God."

When St. Lucy (virgin and martyr) was brought before the pagan judge, who threatened to send her to a brothel to rob her of her virginity, she spoke quite fearlessly to him. The judge was astonished at her courage and asked her for an explanation. She replied: "All who live chaste and devout lives are the temples of the Holy Spirit."

St. Teresa of Avila

This great teacher of the spiritual life wrote beautifully and frequently about this truth. "Try to realize," she says, "that in each of us is a magnificent temple, all built of gold and precious stones, in a word, of a great king who dwells there, and try to realize, because it is true, that you are contributing to this splendor. This temple or palace is your own soul when it is pure, and no palace on earth can rival it in magnificence. The virtues are the diamonds with which it is decorated, and the greater these virtues are, the more sparkling and dazzling are the diamonds. And finally try to remember that in this palace dwells the King of kings, who of His infinite goodness desires to be a Father to you; that He is seated upon a throne of very great price, and that throne is your heart. Such a King is not left alone by His court, but they are always with Him and since they are full of love for us, they pray to Him for us and for our good. If I had known formerly that so great a King dwells in the little palace of my heart, I would not so often have left Him alone there." She adds a bit of practical advice: "One who desires to acquire the habit of living with this kind Master must conquer self by withdrawing his senses into himself; in conversation, in listening, etc., let him remember that there is someone at the bottom of his heart to whom he can speak, listen, etc. Thus, little by little, he will form the habit of never being separated from his divine Companion" *(Way of Perfection,* Ch. 30).

St. Thérèse of Lisieux

The writings of this modern saint, the Little Flower, as she is popularly called, are filled with thoughts about the presence of God in her heart. We select a few of them.

"Jesus comes, and with Him come the other two Persons of the Blessed Trinity, to take possession of our souls. Jesus promised this at the Last Supper."

"I know and I have experienced that the 'kingdom of God is within us.' Our Lord instructs us without the noise of words. I have never heard Him speak, but I know that He is within me. He is always guiding and inspiring me, and, just when I need them, lights hitherto unseen break in upon me. This is not as a rule during prayer, but in the midst of my daily work."

"Yes, I know that when I show charity to others, it is simply Jesus acting in me, and the more closely I am united to Him, the more dearly I love my Sisters."

"Our Lord nourishes me, each moment with food that is ever new. I find it within me, not knowing how it got there. I simply believe it is Jesus hidden in my poor heart who is secretly at work, inspiring me with what He wishes me to do at each moment as the occasion arises."

"I do not know what more I shall have in heaven than I have on earth, for as regards being with God, I am that already on earth."

Finally: "My one interior occupation was to unite myself ever more closely to God, knowing that all else would be given me. And indeed, I have never been disappointed."

Sister Elizabeth of the Trinity

The special mission of this saintly Carmelite who died at Dijon, France, on November 6, 1906, seems to have been to show to what heights of sanctity one can be led by living with God in one's heart. In her various letters we find the following thoughts. "The secret of sanctity is to think that we have heaven within us." "I have found my heaven on earth, for heaven is God, and God is in my soul. On the day I realized this all things were seen by me in a new light." "To forget self is very simple; I will tell you the secret: think of God who dwells within you, whose temple you are. By degrees the soul becomes accustomed to live in His blessed company, realizing that it bears a little heaven within it in which the God of Love has made

His home." "Live with the Three in the heaven of your soul. The Father will overshadow you, making a cloud between you and the things of this world, to keep you all His own. He will communicate His power to you so that you will love Him with a love as strong as death. The Word will imprint in your soul as in a crystal the image of His own beauty, and you will be pure with His purity, luminous with His light. The Holy Spirit will transform you into a mystic lyre. Beneath His divine touch your silence will send forth a magnificent canticle of love." And shortly before her death: "I confide to you the secret which has made my life an anticipated heaven: The belief that a Being whose name is LOVE is dwelling within us at every moment of the day and night, and He asks us to live in His company."

Blessed Arnold Janssen

Blessed Arnold Janssen, who died in 1909, was a zealous and holy priest, the Founder of three religious Congregations for work in the foreign missions. He taught his members the habit of practicing living with God in their hearts by word and example. He himself had resolved: "I will find and worship God in my heart." And that was what he did, from early morning till late at night. He advised his spiritual sons and daughters: "Let us remember the throne of the Triune God in our hearts at the beginning and the end of each day, and when we lie awake at night on our beds. Upon retiring, be mindful of the presence of the entire Blessed Trinity in your hearts. When we lie awake on our beds, let us remember that the Blessed Trinity has its throne in our hearts, and let us adore it."

"We must foster and establish a deep conviction of the indwelling of the Blessed Trinity in the soul by grace. We shall frequently recall this inner presence and bring fervent affections and pleasing sacrifices to the divine Love who has not disdained to come and dwell in our poor hearts."

To remind all of this truth he placed in all the houses of his Congregations clocks or bells which would strike every fifteen minutes, and he composed a set of short acts of faith, hope and charity to be recited in common when the clock struck the quarter hour. At the head of each letter he wrote the words: "May the Most Holy Trinity live in our hearts." He desired all the members to do the same, as a reminder of the presence of God in their hearts.

An Overwhelming Thought

Yes, when we reflect upon this truth in a spirit of deep and living faith—God who is infinite Love, the highest and most lovable Good, really and truly lives in my heart at every moment of the day and night—the thought is truly overwhelming. We should often make an act of profound faith in this truth: God is in my heart. What joy and peace will be mine if I acquire this habit of constantly living in the awareness of the truth that God who loves me ardently is present and living in my heart! Little by little, I must make Him my "Treasure," for then my heart will turn to Him freely and easily. Our Lord said: "Where your treasure is, there will your heart be also."

Pope Leo XIII in his famous letter on the Holy Spirit said: "This wonderful union which is properly called 'Indwelling' differs only in degree or state from that with which God makes the saints happy in heaven."

The Holy Spirit in Our Lives

The Holy Spirit who came to the Church on Pentecost remains in her, and there is no reason He should not do in our day what He did in the early days of the Church. Pope John Paul II says that the Spirit of Christ is "that Holy Spirit promised and continually communicated by the Redeemer and whose descent, which was revealed on the day of Pentecost, endures for ever. Thus the powers of the Spirit, the gifts of the Spirit, and the fruits of the Holy Spirit are revealed in men. The present-day Church seems to repeat with ever greater fervor and with holy insistence: 'Come, Holy Spirit!' Come! Come! 'Heal our wounds, our strength renew; On our dryness pour Your dew; Wash the stains of guilt away; Bend the stubborn heart and will; Melt the frozen, warm the chill; Guide the steps that go astray'" *(Redemptor hominis, 18)*.

It is "the Spirit that gives life—a fountain of water, springing up into life everlasting (cf. John 4:14; 7:38-39); through *Him* the Father restores life to men dead through sin, until one day He will bring their mortal bodies to life in Christ (cf. Romans 8:10-11).

"The Spirit dwells in the Church and in the hearts of the faithful as in a temple (cf. 1 Corinthians 3:16; 6:19) and in them prays and gives evidence of their filial adoption (cf. Galatians 4:6; Romans 8:15-16 and 26). He guides the Church toward all of the truth (cf. John 16:13). He unifies it in communion and in the ministry, He instructs and directs it with different hierarchic and charismatic gifts and embellishes it with His fruits (cf. Ephesians 4:11-12; 1 Corinthians 12:4; Galatians 5:22).

"We must have recourse to Christ's thinking. Christ entrusted the fulfillment of His work among men to *two* different factors: the Holy Spirit and the apostles.... These two missions come equally from Christ. The indisputable design of the divine Founder of the Church intends that the Church be built by the apostles and vivified by the Holy Spirit. The apostles build the body of the Church, whose soul is the Spirit of Christ" (Pope Paul VI, May 18, 1966).

"Do not separate the Spirit from the hierarchy, from the institutional structure of the Church, as if they were two antagonistic expressions of Christianity, or as if one, the Spirit, could be obtained by us without the ministry of the other, the Church, the qualified instrument of truth and grace. It is true that the Spirit 'blows where it will' (John 3:8). But we cannot presume that He will come to us, if we are deliberately absent from the vehicle, chosen by Christ, to communicate Him to us. He who does not adhere to the Body of Christ—we will repeat with St. Augustine—leaves the sphere animated by the Spirit of Christ" (Pope Paul VI, May 26, 1971).

In the Creed of the People of God we pray:

"We believe in the Holy Spirit, who is Lord, and Giver of life, who is adored and glorified together with the Father and the Son. He spoke to us by the prophets; He was sent by Christ after His resurrection and His ascension to the Father; He illuminates, vivifies, protects and guides the Church; He purifies the Church's members if they do not shun His grace. His action, which penetrates to the inmost of the soul, enables man to respond to the call of Jesus: 'Be perfect as your Heavenly Father is perfect' (Mt. 5:48)."

III
THEOLOGICAL EXPLANATION

God's Presence

We say that God is present everywhere but we find it hard to understand this because we are used to thinking of material things—things which can be seen, felt, etc.; things which have length, width, height, thickness, etc. So when we try to think of God as everywhere, like air or space, we just cannot picture Him to ourselves as a person, for the only kind of person we know is the human person which exists in a body and not outside of it. It does not extend beyond it.

But we often speak of material things, also of men, being present to others not just physically, but also by their knowledge and activity. Thus the staff of the control tower of a satellite are present to the crew by instructions, advice, warnings and also at times by direct power, correcting things that have gone wrong or bringing the satellite back to earth.

Similarly, the men in the control tower of an airport are present to the pilots of planes landing and taking off by giving them directions, information about wind, runways, etc., for safe landings.

The sun is said to be present on the earth by its light and warmth, because by this activity it gives life and growth to plants and animals and exerts its influence in many other ways. Again, it is said to be more present in some places than in others, that is, at the equator, rather than at the poles, because of its greater activity there.

In a similar way, God is present by His knowledge and power, but He is also present by His very being (essence), and in this He is unlike the man in the tower or the sun in the sky. They are not actually or really present where they are active, but only where they are physically.

God, since He is a spirit and not a material being, has no parts, no extension, no dimensions of any kind. So God does not occupy or fill space in a material way. Spirits are present in space by their activity. They are where they are active, where they are using their power. So my soul is present whole and entire in every part of my body, simply because it is active in every part, even my fingertips.

So God is said to be everywhere by His being, knowledge and power, because He knows and controls, keeps all things in existence, and exercises His knowledge and power everywhere. In this way, God is intimately present to all things, though His presence is greater in some than others.

Kinds of Presence

When we speak of being present we usually mean being near to someone or something, though not in it.

God is not only near but also in all things, though in some more than in others. He is said to be more or less in them by the measure of His activity. Thus, He is present in lifeless things—stones, water, etc.—because He keeps them in existence. He is more present in plants because He is giving them life; still more present in animals because He gives them feeling and movement, and still more present in human beings because He is more active in them, giving them intelligence and free will in the natural order, and even divine life in the supernatural order.

An Example

Let us take an example. A young man and a young woman live in the same apartment house, but do not know each other. As time goes on they meet occasionally and exchange greetings. Friendship develops and eventually they marry. Now they are present to each other not merely physically as at the beginning, when they were merely living in the same building, but much more intimately, in head and heart, in mind and will, as husband and wife.

They are the same persons as they were at the beginning, but now they are present to each other in an entirely new way by their intimate and delicate knowledge and love of each other—a love which constantly tries to show itself in a thousand little attentions, refinements, delicacies; a love which instinctively goes to excesses, even to follies. Nothing suffices to express the depth and intensity of their love, for "Love is blind and lovers do not see the follies that adorn their loving."

But the excessive follies of lovers are as nothing when compared with the delicacy and refinements of God's love for each one of us. No detail is too insignificant to escape His attention. God living in our hearts is all eagerness for our very best interests, especially those that concern our eternal welfare, everlasting happiness. But even here on earth He wishes to live most intimately with me and me with Him. If we only had a deep, living Faith in this tremendous truth of God's delicate love for each of us personally, we would trust in Him without limits and love Him unto folly, for "love is repaid by love alone," as St. Thérèse points out.

God's Special Presence in Us

The special presence of God in our hearts is something much deeper, something much more intimate, for it is a knowledge and love of God as He is in Himself, a knowledge through faith and a union through love.

The Holy Spirit, who comes to us gives us a share in the divine life, is continually at work to bring us to our divine inheritance as children of God and heirs of heaven. God who is a Spirit can be intimately present to man, an intelligent and free being, only by knowledge and love, and the deeper this love is, the more intimate and greater is His presence and the greater His activity. So when we speak of the presence of God in our hearts, as far as His being or physical presence is concerned, it is not different from that in all things, but there is a tremendous difference in His presence in the soul as its Sanctifier through sanctifying grace. In a soul not in sanctifying grace He is said not to be present, i.e., in this special way, since He is not active in giving and preserving the divine life. But He is present only in the general sense in which He is present to creatures as their Creator and Preserver.

Adopted Children of God

We are called adopted children of God. Let us try to explain this by a little story to understand how far God's love for us goes. A skillful doctor, while passing through a remote village in the bush, comes across an abandoned infant, all covered with sores and all but starved to death. He feels sorry for it, picks it up, and takes it home with him. There he personally cares for it most tenderly, giving many hours of his own time, buying most costly medicines, and even gives it a blood transfusion of his own blood, to preserve its life and bring it back to health. As time goes on, it becomes strong and healthy. He makes the child a member of his own family, cares for it, educates it as he does his own children, giving it equal rights with them to an inheritance.

God in His merciful love and compassion has done all this and much more for each of us. The doctor could only give his blood to help the child, but even this and the adoption of the child could not make him its real father—he could not give it his own life, for that was received from the child's parents from whom it was born. But God has given us a share in His own divine life as God, so that we are really and truly children of God. He did not treat us "just as if" we were His children, but He actually did give us a share in His own life. He is truly "Our Father." Only God could do such a thing. The Second Person of the Blessed Trinity is what we call the natural Son of God, and we are said to be God's adopted children, because we share in the divine life by participation, but it is a participation in the very life of God Himself. Our divine adoption does far more than mere human or legal adoption. We *are* children of God. St. John exclaims in astonishment: "Behold, what manner of love the Father has for us that we should be called children of God, and that we actually are" (1 John 3:1). God's love for each of us personally, individually, combines all that is best in the love of the best fathers and mothers, brothers and sisters, brides and bridegrooms, dearest and truest friends. God's love for us is all this and infinitely more! And *He* is present in our hearts, yes, in *my* heart!

Possessing and Possessed

It is this special presence of God in us that makes us possess God and God possess us. We are possessed by God and we also possess Him. In the case of the young man and woman mentioned above, who though physically present to each other were strangers at the beginning, as bridegroom and bride, they became intimately and mutually present and possessed each other in thought and love, in heart and affection. In a similar way, God is present in us through knowledge and love which the Holy Spirit diffuses in our hearts. The electric current is in the wires of the electric light bulb; it possesses them, but it is also possessed by them. Similarly, a sponge steeped in water is totally possessed by the water and also fully possesses the water. So God is said to possess us and to be possessed by us.

This presence of God in our heart is not a greater physical nearness, but it consists in this intimate relation of knowledge and love which causes Him to be in us and us in Him. No natural intimacy of earthly kind—not even that of bride and bridegroom—can even remotely compare with this union between God and ourselves, God in our heart. This change takes place in Baptism, when the Holy Spirit gives us sanctifying grace, the life of God. As we think deeply of this it is almost breathtaking to realize how deeply and tenderly God loves us. He is with us in our heart at every moment of the day and night!

Activity of God in My Heart

God the Father, Son, and Holy Spirit, all three Divine Persons are present, living in my heart as the "Soul's Sweet Guest." But God is not only at home there as a delightful Guest. He is very active there. In what way? What is it that He is doing in us? From what has already been said, we can see that He cares for us with the greatest watchfulness in all that concerns our body and soul in the natural and supernatural order. Nothing is too insignificant; nothing escapes His eye. But His chief activity is concerned with the deepening of our divine life, by increasing grace and all the virtues, especially those which unite us with Himself—faith, hope, love—and those which put us right with our fellowmen—love, justice, prudence, fortitude, temperance. And through His seven gifts and twelve fruits, He makes us more docile to His holy will; and He gives us a taste of the bliss of the beatitudes.* In a word, His activity consists in preparing us for eternal happiness in heaven, by transforming us more and more as members of Christ into a living image of our divine Head, Jesus Himself, the Son "in whom the Father was well pleased." We remind ourselves of this in the Third Eucharistic Prayer of the Mass: "Father, all life, all holiness comes from you, through your Son Jesus Christ by the working of the Holy Spirit." Truly, God is working wonderful things within us, not only drawing us more and more closely to Himself, but by making us more and more one with Himself, so that we become capable of sharing in His own happiness as God for all eternity: "Enter into the joy of your Lord!"

---

*See *Appendix*.

IV
DUTIES TO GOD IN THE TEMPLE OF OUR HEART

St. Paul repeatedly called the attention of the early Christians to this duty. And he pointed out the consequences of the presence of the Holy Spirit in the temple of their bodies. Briefly, these are three: carefully guard and protect this temple, beautify it, and enter it often. We shall say just a few words about each.

Guard This Temple

St. Paul told his converts that they should not "extinguish the Spirit." "If anyone will desecrate the temple of God, God will destroy him" (1 Corinthians 3:17). We are shocked when beautiful churches or even cathedrals are ruthlessly destroyed and desecrated. But when we commit mortal sin, we do far worse to God's temple within us, in our heart. Mortal sin is a serious offense against God's law. Earthly temples can be rebuilt by men, but only God can rebuild the temple in our heart if we destroy it. When we were baptized, the priest said: "Depart, unclean spirit and make way for the Spirit of God." When we commit sin, we reverse the command and say: "Depart, Holy Spirit of God, and make way for Satan, the unclean spirit." We literally throw God, our most loving Father, out of His own house. That is an awful thing to do. St. Paul calls it "crucifying anew the Son of God, trampling underfoot the precious blood of Christ" (Hebrews 10:29). "He who insults the Spirit of grace will be condemned to a far more severe punishment" (Ibid.).

But St. Paul also said that his converts should "not grieve the Holy Spirit." We do this when we commit venial sin, for we deface and damage God's temple in our heart. We make it an unpleasant place for Him to stay in by the mean way in which we treat Him, by not caring about filth and dirt which we heap up and even by the contempt with which we treat Him. We must carefully guard and protect God's temple in our heart.

Beautify This Temple

The richer the ornaments, decorations, windows, etc., of a beautiful church, the more attractive it is. The ornaments of God's temple in our heart are the virtues with which God delights in seeing it adorned.* We know quite well what these virtues are, so we need not speak here at length about them.

---

*See Appendix.

Often Enter This Temple

When a very dear friend visits us, we do not let him sit alone for hours in our house without having a word with him. God is surely much more than even our very dearest friend on earth. We should remember that He is living with and in us at all times, at every moment of the day and night, and so we should often enter into conversation with Him. We should try to speak to Him with the simplicity and filial trust of a little child to its father. In this way we grow in a living faith in His presence within our heart, and turning to Him, we often enter this temple, until it gradually become a habit with us to live with Him there, so that we are "on fire with the Holy Spirit."

V
INTIMACY

By His activity within us God wishes to build up between Himself and us a tender, astounding familiarity. But we must not become discouraged because it does not come at once. St. Thérèse wrote to one of her missionary brothers: "I am not surprised that you find it hard to be familiar with Jesus—one does not become so in a day." But we must persevere in our efforts. Two things are required: we must remove the obstacles to intimacy and make good use of the means of arriving at it.

Obstacles to Intimacy

The obstacles may all be put under one heading: lack of interior purity. We must strive for a fourfold purity.

1. *Will.* We must strive to have a pure conscience. This we do by giving our will entirely to God. This means that we must avoid not only all mortal sins, but also all deliberate venial sins, especially those which are habitual or due to negligence. In-

dividual or occasional falls, which are not due to sheer carelessness or negligence, and of which we repent promptly and sincerely do us little or no harm. We must love God with our *whole* soul.

2. *Mind.* Dissipation of mind is also a serious obstacle. We must not let our thoughts wander about at random, but must control them, not only those which are sinful or dangerous—especially uncharitableness, unwillingness to forgive, etc.—but also those which are innocent in themselves, but more or less useless and distracting. We must love God with our *whole* mind.

3. *Heart.* Our excessive attachments are a third obstacle. We must courageously cut ourselves loose from all undue attachment to persons, places, things, etc., which draw our affections away from God. These make us divide our love between God and creatures. We must love God with our *whole* heart.

4. *Actions.* Self-seeking is a fourth obstacle. We must not seek ourselves, but God in all our actions, that is, in all the acts of the faculties of our soul and of the senses of our body. In all these we must seek only God's good pleasure. We must love God with our *whole* strength.

The more we work for this fourfold purification by mortification and self-denial, the more we remove the obstacles that stand in the way of intimacy and the more we shall grow in the awareness of God's presence in our heart. Our intimacy, our familiarity with God in our heart, will be in proportion to the efforts made for this fourfold purity, for the removal of the obstacles.

Means to Intimacy

In removing the obstacles, in striving for this four-fold purity, we must use positive means, which help us to grow in this intimacy. Among these we mention the following.

Childlike Faith

We should often make deep, living acts of childlike faith in this truth that God is really and truly present in our heart. The best way of making these little acts of faith is to do so in our own words by little ejaculations, telling God that we believe He is really present in our heart, that we are convinced of this truth, that we give Him thanks, adore Him, ask His help, etc. When our Blessed Mother held the Infant Jesus in her hands, when she stood beneath the cross, she too did not see anything to show that Jesus was God, yet she believed it most firmly. These acts of faith are very important for us if we wish to develop the habit of remembering the presence of God within us.

Deep Humility

Living faith in the real presence of God in our hearts leads us to true humility. We think of who He is and what we are, and we are filled with awe and reverence. We are more careful to avoid all sin and all that which will displease Him. We humble ourselves for our faults, but never let them discourage us as long as we sincerely wish and strive to overcome them.

Filial Trust

God, our Father, knows our weakness far better than we ourselves do, but He also knows our good will and our good resolutions. So we must never lose our trust in Him, for He is infinitely merciful, always ready to forgive. He loves us most tenderly and cares for us far better than the best father or mother could care for their only child. St. Thérèse said: "We can never have too much confidence in God. He is so good, so mighty, so merciful. We shall receive from Him quite as much as we hope for. What wounds Jesus, what hurts Him to the heart is lack of trust in Him."

Ardent, Generous Love of God

Since God who abides in our heart loves us so much, we should make Him a return of love. Without love, even the greatest, the most difficult work, the most painful sufferings have little or no value, but with intense love, even the least things take on great value with God. St. Thérèse said: "The least act of pure love is worth more than all other works," that is, those done with less love of God. Again she says: "If you were too lazy to pick up a piece of thread from the floor, but still did it for the love of God, you may save a soul." Love gives such value to little things, and love helps us to make sacrifices, to overcome ourselves.

Recollection

Recollection, or silence of the mind, does not come by itself. It requires persistent effort on our part, for our mind is continually active.

If we look into ourselves we shall see that often, almost always, when we are alone, we are carrying on a conversation with ourselves, not (usually) in words, but in our thoughts. Our mind and imagination are continually active. Well, instead of this conversation with ourselves—talking to and with ourselves—we must learn to talk to God within us. We must train ourselves by earnest efforts to do this. This means that we must learn to keep silence, to practice recollection or silence of the mind: the control of our thoughts, memory, and imagination.

This is impossible unless we keep strict control of the doors and windows of our mind, our eyes and ears, curbing our instinctive curiosity to see and hear everything. Even things which are innocent in themselves—such as news, the radio, etc., can be a source of much distraction, when sought merely for the sake of pleasure. Our mind is like a mill which grinds continually and it grinds whatever is put into it. We must decide what will and what will not be fed into it. This we do by strict control of the channels—our eyes and ears. The mind that is perpetually occupied with external things has no room or time for the thought of God in the heart. But by practice, the habit of recollection will be formed, and it will not be too difficult to turn our thoughts again and again to God in our heart—during work, recreation, etc. Thus, we shall find ourselves living with God in our heart at all hours of the day and night. As a magnet draws bits of iron to itself, so God, our Magnet in our heart, will draw our thoughts and affections to Himself, gently, yet powerfully. He will have become our "treasure," and in us will be fulfilled the words of our Lord: "Where your treasure is, there is your heart also." Then we shall "find rest for our souls."

Docility to the Holy Spirit

It becomes easier for us to say "Yes" to God's holy will made known to us by our daily duties and the events of life, to be docile to Him and easily led by Him, if we remember that it is He who sends these things and that He is in our heart. This disposition of docility is the shortest way to intimacy with God in our heart.

Mary, Our Model and Helper

Spiritual writers teach that the surest, shortest, easiest and most perfect way to Jesus and to holiness is through Mary, His Mother (St. Louis Marie Grignon de Montfort). She is the model of a life of union with God in our heart, not only because for nine months she was the living tabernacle of the Son of God made flesh in her virginal womb and lived with Him visibly for thirty years at Nazareth, but also because after His Ascension, she lived a life of most intimate recollection and union with the Father, Son, and Holy Spirit abiding in her heart. Never was there a deeper union, never a more intimate living with God. But, as we know, she is not only our model, but also our powerful helper. Mary is most eager to assist us in all our efforts for holiness, and hence in our efforts to cultivate this filial intimacy, this amazing familiarity, with God the Father, Son and Holy Spirit in our heart. Our confidence in her cannot even remotely approach the eagerness of her desire to help us reach our goal and find our rest in God abiding in our heart. Jesus came to us by the overshadowing of the Holy Spirit through Mary, and through her He leads us to Him.

The Holy Eucharist

While all these means to intimacy are helpful, the greatest and most powerful of all is the Holy Eucharist. In the Sacrifice of the Mass, no matter what method we personally may use in offering it, the most important thing is the interior disposition of being one with Christ the High Priest and Victim offered there, the willingness to be entirely His, to be one with Him.

Holy Communion is the great sacrament which not merely unites us with Christ, but makes us one with Him, transforms us little by little until it is He who not only abides in or is present in us, but also lives in us in our mind and will. Holy Communion is the great sacrament of oneness, which makes us die to self, so that Christ may live in us. The more we die and are crucified to ourselves, to our natural likes and dislikes, the more perfectly He can and will live in us. Then, we shall use all the means mentioned here far more fruitfully and effectively, and live in an astounding familiarity with God in our heart.

VI
ACTUALLY LIVING WITH GOD IN MY HEART

Much of what was said about the means of intimacy is already actually living with God in our heart and leads to familiarity with Him. It will be well worth all the sacrifices needed to prepare the way: removal of the obstacles by working hard for the fourfold purity of soul, mind, heart and action and by using the means which will help to reach this interior purity. Actually living with God in my heart reaches into every corner of my life from early morning till late at night, yes, even from night till morning. In this way, little by little, we grow in the awareness of God living in us until it becomes a kind of second nature and we live with Him as if we saw and felt Him present at all times and in all places.

Cardinal Newman

Cardinal Newman describes a Christian—not a priest or a religious—as a person absorbed by the presence of God in his heart, one who lives always with the thought "God dwells in me." We must grow in the awareness of this presence of God within us. There is no truly Christian life, above all, no interior life without it.

God's Atmosphere

We must keep in mind who God is—how infinitely lovable He is both for His own sake as the highest, supreme Good, and for the immense love which He has for each one of us personally, individually. He is the best, most loving and understanding of Fathers. We must remind ourselves again and again that it is *He* who abides in us.

In the spiritual life it can easily happen that we become feverishly excited about our work and completely absorbed in it, in what we are doing, even though our work is holy and we work for God. While doing the work of God we may unconsciously slip into carrying it out from mere natural or human motives, if we are not on our guard. How can we avoid this? By surrounding ourselves with God's atmosphere.

Our earth, in its orbit around the sun, while revolving at the same time on its own axis, travels hundreds of thousands of miles at a tremendous speed, and yet no one notices any disturbances or sudden changes, because it carries its own atmosphere with it. For us spiritually, our sun-illuminated atmosphere is the presence of the All-Good God in our heart. The remembrance of this will help us to judge all things at their true value. It will help us to keep calm when everything seems to go wrong, and prevent all feverish haste and excited activity. It will help us to do our duty faithfully and to keep our intention pure. It will bring us greater peace. God's atmosphere, sometimes called living in His presence, is an oft-repeated and loving remembrance of His presence in our heart. St. Thérèse lived in such an atmosphere, for she says that scarcely three minutes passed without a loving thought of God. She said: "We read that the Israelites, while building the walls of Jerusalem, worked with one hand and held a sword in the other. That is an image of what we should do: work conscientiously, but with perfect freedom and detachment of heart."

The Pause that Refreshes

In one of its advertisements, the Coca-Cola Company pictures a group of travelers resting and drinking a bottle of Coca-Cola. Above the picture are the words: "The Pause that Refreshes." The thought finds even deeper application to the thought of God's presence within us. From morning until night, in whatever we may be doing, but especially when we are under pressure from worry, anxiety, work, or whatever it may be, a pause to think of the intimate presence of God who is Love within us can indeed be "the pause that refreshes."

Listening to God

Spiritual writers tell us that we should listen to God in prayer. But God speaks to us outside of prayer in many ways. In fact, He is speaking to us all the time, during the day and the night. But we are not listening to what He wants to tell us. For this we need a deep faith, a firm belief that He is talking to us in many ways. If we want to listen to a program on the radio, first we must turn on the radio; we must also tune in to the right station; we must be on the right wave length to get the program we want. We do this spiritually by silence and recollection. Then we shall hear God speaking to us in many ways, some of which are the following:

a) *Usual ways.* When we read the Holy Scriptures, especially the Gospels, or spiritual books, in spiritual conferences, retreats, advice given to us, reproofs or corrections, etc.—if we do these things with distractions or negligence, we do not hear Him—we are not tuned in.

b) *Our duties.* God clearly tells us what He wants us to do. He tells us by the commandments; by the duties of our vocation; if we are religious by our holy Rule, daily order, commands of superiors, etc. But we must be tuned in to recognize His voice.

c) *Events of each passing minute.* With God nothing happens by accident, for nothing escapes His vigilance or power. All comes from His Providence. His hand is in everything. There are things which affect many people—such as floods, lightnings, cyclones, storms, etc. Some affect us personally—such as accidents, sickness, failures, crosses, temptations, etc. Some come from other men—such as criticism, slander, calumny, physical harm, damage to our property, etc.; sometimes from their stupidity or ignorance; sometimes also from their malice, from lack of sympathy, etc. Some come to us also from our personal limitations—physical, intellectual or even spiritual—such as poor sight, hearing, nervousness, dullness, etc. (Quite often these seeming handicaps are a safeguard, planned by God for our protection.)

d) *God's voice in nature.* His wonderful perfections in the visible world: sun, moon, stars,...mountains and valleys, oceans and rivers,...the great variety of trees, flowers, vegetables, each with their own kinds of seed; the animals, birds, fish, etc.—the largest to the tiniest things are so many voices speaking to us about God's infinite Wisdom, Power, Love—if we are tuned in.

God speaks to us by these things not by words which strike our ears, but by the thoughts which He puts into our minds, by the affections He puts into our hearts. If we train ourselves to listen we shall gradually find that He is speaking to us always and everywhere.

Man-made Reminders

In our efforts to remember the presence of God in our heart, especially at the beginning, we shall find man-made reminders not only useful, but perhaps even necessary. Their sight can help us to bring back our thoughts again and again to God within us. One religious attached a safety pin to the cuff of his sleeve. It did not serve any evident purpose there. When he was asked about it: Was it readiness for an emergency?..., he smiled as he replied: "Safety first! Don't forget God is with you in your heart." Such a reminder can be almost anything we choose. But usually it will be necessary to change it from time to time, for otherwise it will cease to be a reminder. Seeing it constantly will become routine and it will no longer be a reminder. Gradually, awareness of God in our heart will become habitual and there will be no need of man-made reminders.

In Prayer

Many of our distractions in prayer are due to the fact that we begin abruptly, without thinking of what we are about to do. Devoutly making the sign of the cross—recalling that the Father, Son, and Holy Spirit to whom we are about to speak, are present in us—will help much to fix our attention at the start and to control our thoughts during our prayers, especially the shorter ones. In longer prayers we can recall the thought of God's presence from time to time and bring back our scattered thoughts to Him.

Little pauses in our prayer are also helpful to recall ourselves. The Church puts such pauses in various parts of the liturgy just for this purpose; otherwise, even the liturgy can become quite mechanical, a matter of routine. In our prayers it is good for us to pause in order to listen to what God may have to say to us. Often a simple look with faith at the tabernacle, a crucifix, a picture of the Blessed Virgin Mary, are enough to hear His voice. In time, we find ourselves united with Him without words at all, without direct thoughts or affections, but simply heart to heart.

The Gardener of Ars

The gardener of Ars is an example of this. The story is told in the life of St. John Vianney. A simple, uneducated gardener of his parish, who worked in his garden until mid-afternoon, would stop at the church on his way home, put his tools in the vestibule and enter the church. He would spend two or three hours there. St. John Vianney noticed that he never read from a book, did not use a rosary, or even move his lips. He just knelt or sat there looking at the taber- nacle. His face was a picture of deep peace and con- tentment. One day the saint asked his parishioner what he did during those long hours. The gardener felt embarrassed and confused, for he did not know what to reply, for he said nothing, asked for nothing, did not even think of anything. Finally, he said sim- ply: "I look at Him, and He looks at me, and we are both happy." That was prayer of a very high order— prayer without words, even without thoughts, but deep in the heart.

During Work

All of us have our work to do. It may be in the home—domestic work of all kinds—or it may be in the shop, factory, office, school, on the farm...any- where. To do it well, we must keep our mind on what we are doing and put our best effort into it. We can do this best if we do our work with God, speaking to Him, asking His help, light, etc., as needs arise. When all goes well, we thank Him for His blessing; when diffi- culties arise, we turn to Him, and also when we fail we accept it as the cross, which eventually will bear even richer fruits, for "in the cross is salvation." In the midst of our work, then, we should often remind our- selves of God's presence in our heart.

The Duties of Daily Life

By the holy will of God our daily life is filled with many little duties. It is not always easy for us to conform ourselves to God's plans in these duties of each day. Often we are obliged to make painful sacrifices to overcome ourselves in what He wills from us. His presence in our heart and the assurance it gives us of His help will be our strength. But if we have not formed the habit of turning to Him, if we never even think of His presence within us, we deprive ourselves of all this help and strength. To work for God, we must learn to work with God. Then we shall know from personal experience how true it is that "In His holy will is all our peace." "I have remained in your presence, you have held my right hand" (Ps. 73:23).

In Anxiety and Fears

Sometimes we worry about the past, our falls, confessions, etc., even though we have tried to be sincere about everything. But the past should be left fully to the infinitely merciful love of God with utter trust, knowing how boundless is His desire for our eternal happiness. Souls are lost only by their perverse rejection of the grace of God or by their utter negligence of it. We must never allow the past to stand between God and ourselves or prevent us from a life of intimacy with Him in our heart.

Fears for the future can depress us—fear of things which may, perhaps will, happen to us personally—sickness, loss of work or of property; serious temptation, or other spiritual trials. But the future is in God's hands and is safer there than if it were in our own, for

He loves us much more than we could truly love ourselves. We know St. Paul's words: "God works all things for the good of those who love Him," and Saint Augustine adds: "yes, even our sins." In a spirit of childlike trust we must leave everything to His watchful Providence and in a spirit of simple faith accept His guidance in all those events of the future. He loves us and lives in our heart, so why should we fear? Our attitude to the unknown future should always be "Your will be done!" or to quote St. Augustine again: "Give me the grace to do what You command and then command what You will!" Deep faith in the abiding presence of God in our heart leads to utter, filial, trustful abandonment to God in all things because we know that He loves us.

In Difficulties and Crosses

Crosses in some form or another, sometimes small, sometimes large, heavy, and lasting for years are the lot of many followers of Christ. Each day brings its own little basket of crosses. To bear them fruitfully we need help. Such help can come from the thought of God in our heart, for they come to us through Him and without Him they would not be placed on our weak shoulders. Every one of these crosses is selected precisely for us and sent to us at the right time by Him. Through them He wishes to draw us closer to Himself. We are not sparrows, or wild flowers. We are His children, so we can be sure of much greater care than is given to them. With Him, as we said before, nothing happens by accident, noth-

ing escapes His watchful attention. He rules everything from His abode in the center of our heart. The
thought of this helps us to turn to Him with childlike
trust and complete oneness with His holy will, even
though at present we may not see the *why* of His
ways of dealing with us. Our life is made up of many
seemingly disconnected bits and pieces, and we fail to
see any kind of planning or order in them. The events
of each day are like the many-shaped pieces of a
jigsaw puzzle: they seem to have no purpose and do
not fit together at all; they seem to have no unified
plan, yet every piece fits, and if even one would be
changed ever so slightly, it would detract from the
perfection of the whole picture. We recall the stories
of Job, of Joseph in Egypt, of Tobias, and we see how
every difficulty, even from the injustice of man, was
fitted by God into the final and completed picture of
the divine blessing. Thus God also sees the plan He
has for each of us, and when we see it completed in
heaven we shall be astounded and sincerely thankful
to God for the wisdom, power, and especially love by
which He directed every little detail of our lives so as
to bring us to heaven and the great reward He has in
store there for us. For the present we must live by
faith, blind but utterly firm, and by abandonment to
His holy will. All this comes more easily if we have
formed the habit of living with Him in our heart.

In Temptations

Even our Lord was tempted severely and
repeatedly. None of us can expect to be entirely free
from temptation from some source or other. Our

temptations may be severe, stubborn, very persistent and seemingly beyond our strength, but we have within us One who is stronger than all the powers of darkness. If we turn to our heavenly Father in our heart with simple, sincere and humble trust, we shall be given the strength we need to struggle even to exhaustion, but to win in the end. "I can do all things in him who strengthens me," said St. Paul. We need but cry out with confidence, "Guard me as the pupil of your eye; hide me in the shadow of your wings" (Psalm 17).

Our Daily Falls and Faults

One of our greatest temptations is discouragement because of our falls in spite of our good will and earnest efforts. We become depressed and have no more energy to keep trying. But if our faults are not habitual or due to sheer laziness or negligence, we need not lose heart. They serve God's purpose of grounding us in humility more and more, by making us realize our helplessness and need of divine help. For this reason God leaves some weaknesses even in great saints. God does not require that we succeed, but that we make the serious effort to succeed. Success is His gift which He bestows as He sees best for us.

God looks to our interior attitude, to our sincere desire to avoid these faults, and He is well pleased with this. Our faults used properly become stepping-stones to an even deeper union with Him in trust and love. For this we need only make proper use of them by turning to Him promptly, humbly, and sincerely with full trust, asking for His forgiveness. We only have to recall the parables of the lost sheep or prodigal son to know how He reacts to such conduct on our part.

Of this St. Thérèse speaks beautifully and repeatedly: "The Heart of Jesus thrills with joy when He has to deal with all those who truly love, and who, after each little fault, come to fling themselves into His arms imploring forgiveness. He says to His angels what the father said to the servants....

"He knows the faults will be committed again, but cannot reject such a trustful appeal to His love."

Our faults and falls will not discourage us if we learn to live with God in our hearts.

At Meals

Such a homely thing as eating and drinking can also lead me to God in my heart. Recollection at the short prayer before and after meals and especially making the sign of the cross devoutly instead of in a routine and mechanical way will turn our thoughts inward with thanks to God for His gifts. The thought of the many who go hungry will cause us to breathe a prayer for them; the thought of the vinegar and gall offered to our Lord in His awful thirst on the cross will help us to practice a little self-denial also. Thus, caring for this bodily necessity will also draw us nearer to God in our heart. St. Paul did not think it too small or material a thing to offer to God: "Whether you eat or drink, or whatsoever else you do, do all for the glory of God."

At Recreation

We know the saying about the bow that is always bent, and we are all familiar with "All work and no play makes Jack a dull boy." We all need relaxation of mind and body from time to time. Even our Lord sought it repeatedly for Himself and for His Apostles. No matter what form of recreation, whether it be to our liking or a sacrifice of our liking for the pleasure of others, we must try to do our part to give pleasure to others rather than seek it for ourselves by insisting on our own will in the choice or form, for we gain nothing by self-seeking. The thought of God in our heart, as our Companion also at recreation, will make it both for ourselves and if we are in a group also for others, innocent fun and enjoyment, which prepares for us renewed energy for the work that lies ahead. Recreation is also a part of the "whatsoever else you do" of St. Paul.

Love of Our Neighbor

God is present in our neighbor. In any case our Lord gave us the commandment—and He calls it "My commandment" because it is most dear to Him—and He also says: "What you do to the least of my brothers, you do to me." He lives in our neighbor just as He lives in us, though it may be in many different degrees. So what we do to our neighbor in thought or word, deed or omission, we do to Him, whether it be good or evil. Faith helps us to realize this and to serve and love Him in everyone with whom we come into contact, but especially in the poorest and most needy, the suffering and the afflicted.

Zeal for Souls

There are billions of people who do not yet know of God's love, who have never yet heard even the name of our Savior, yet God sincerely wants all of them to come to the eternal joy He has prepared for them. We prove our love for God by our zeal for their salvation. How? St. Thérèse says: "By our little acts of charity, practiced as it were in the dark (secretly), hidden from the eyes of men, we obtain the conversion of the heathen, help missionaries, and gain for them plentiful alms, building in this way spiritual and material temples for our Eucharistic Lord."

Resting in God

Most of us do not sleep so soundly that we do not wake up at night. When we awaken, we can turn our thoughts to God, who is with us in our heart also during the hours of the night, and thus we show Him that we do not forget Him, but as the psalmist puts it, to "Muse on you during the hours of the night," especially if we cannot sleep because we are kept awake by worries, problems or pains which make sleep impossible, and the night an eternity. We can find some little strength and comfort by turning to God in our heart and putting before Him the things that are keeping us from sleep. Peace and sleep come to us, and at times also the solution of the problems which have been the cause of our sleeplessness.

Patience with Ourselves

These are some of the ways of living with God in our heart. We do not arrive at this at once, but only by constant struggle and persevering effort, so we must never grow weary. There are many degrees of this awareness, and we need not lose heart if we do not reach the highest.

We have all experienced the truth of the saying: "The daily becomes commonplace." For instance, if people go to Rome only once and see the Pope, they retain a sharp and lasting memory of that visit. But people who live in Rome and have seen him often and can see him many times do not feel the same, though they have not lost their reverence for him. If you see a fine movie once, you are impressed, moved, enthusiastic. But if you have seen it six or seven times, it no longer affects you in the same way. So it is also with many things of the spiritual order—Holy Mass, Communion, the Real Presence, and with the thought of God in your heart. Even after the newness wears off, we must continue, for this awareness bears its fruit independently of the feeling of God's presence in our heart or the absence of this feeling.

We must not become discouraged. St. Thérèse reminds us again and again that holiness does not consist in prayers, penances, sacraments, external practices of piety, and, above all, not in feelings, but in an interior attitude or disposition of habitual total oneness with God's holy will. It is this disposition that we must try to preserve at all times, living with God in our heart always and everywhere in total, trustful self-surrender, the crowning proof of our love.

When the Sun Hides

In nature the weather is not always the same, but most of the days have normally good weather. But there are also dark, dreary, rainy, chilly days, and they do not depend upon our making. We cannot change them. Sometimes, too, there are severe thunder storms, strong winds, cyclones, floods, earthquakes, etc., but these are exceptions. Then, there are days that are exceptionally beautiful and bright.

The spiritual weather of our soul-life is much the same. Most of the time things go their usual way peacefully. Here and there passing moods settle upon us; we are physically indisposed, depressed, or it may be that at times really severe storms of temptation break over us. But they too pass. Here and there we also have a few hours, even a day or more on the heights of Mount Tabor, and like St. Peter we say, "Lord, it is good for me to be here." But this foretaste of heaven disappears and we must return to our usual life. We have all experienced these changes.

We must learn to live in what spiritual writers call "naked faith," that is, faith stripped of all feelings of consolation, of the sense of the presence of God, etc. In such hours, perhaps even days and weeks of deep desolation and frustration we must cling to God by sheer "naked faith," by faith which is deprived of all its supports, faith in spite of the absolute darkness in which we are steeped. We must believe without a shadow of doubt in God's continuing love for us personally and throw ourselves blindly and trustfully into His arms in the depths of our heart. God is purifying us of our secret self-love by hiding Himself. But the darkness will pass, the morning will come, and the sun will shine with greater brilliance than ever before.

To Sum Up

The ideal is expressed in the following thoughts adapted from *My Father's Will,* by McGariggle, S.J., p. 141: The mother's hands tenderly arrange everything for her infant: they clothe it, feed it, fondle it, do everything lovingly for it. But no mother's care could even remotely come near to the tender and most intimate care of God for every atom of our being, for every incident affecting us, for every association with persons whose lives cross ours in the weaving of history. Our character, our surroundings, and all that affects us, yes, also our limitations, all come to us directly off the hand of God, not only hovering over us more immensely concerned about us than the best of mothers could be for her only child, but really and truly present, abiding in our heart. This should be our habitual frame of mind as normal Christians. It is in such a presence of God that we must submissively and confidently walk the ways of life if we wish to have Christian hearts. This is what it means to live with God in our heart.

A Word of Admonition

Living with God in our heart does not mean actual thinking of Him at all times, at every moment of the day. This is impossible here on earth, and to attempt it would cause a mental breakdown, or would make one a nervous wreck. There must be no overstraining of the mind to practice recollection, but little by little we must accustom ourselves to a simple, oft-repeated and loving remembrance of God in our heart. Gradually, this awareness will grow, and in due time it will become more or less habitual—the thought of God living in our heart will never be far from our consciousness. As we grow in the knowledge and love of God through Mass, the sacraments, prayer, reading of the Gospels, etc., God will mean more and more to us, He will become our "Treasure" which will draw our thoughts more and more to Himself as the great object of the love of our heart. The absence of a feeling of joy or of His presence should not disturb us in the least. In this kind of life there is an unfelt joy and peace, so deep down in the soul that nothing can disturb it. It is the "peace which the world cannot give" —the peace of Christ.

VII
FRUITS OF THIS LIFE

The fruits of this life are a deep peace and joy, a peace and joy not of this world. St. Paul speaks of these fruits and gives a list of them—he calls them fruits of the Spirit—in his letter to the Galatians: "The Spirit brings love, joy, peace, patience, kindness, goodness, fruitfulness, gentleness, continency, chastity..." (Gal. 5:21).

The psalmist chooses the picture of a contented child, sleeping peacefully on its mother's breast: "I keep myself tranquil and quiet, as contented as a nursed child sleeping on its mother's knees" (Ps. 131).

Speaking of this, Father William Gier, a deeply spiritual priest, says: "The thought consoles me: wherever I go or live, God is with me. Whether I live or die, God is with me. He is the constant witness of my whole interior and exterior activity, no matter what men may think or say of me. If I am honored, whether deserved or undeserved, God is my witness; He knows it all. If I am looked upon with suspicion, whether with or without reason, God is my witness; He knows all. Are men my friends or my enemies? He is my witness. I am what I am in His sight, nothing more and nothing less, regardless of men's appraisal. Lovingly He helps me from His throne in my heart. I wish never to lose sight of Him in all my thoughts, desires, words, deeds, sufferings: to live with Him in my heart."

Special Fruits

Fidelity to this practice may dispose us to receive special gifts of a higher order, of the mystical order. Speaking of these, Blosius, a renowned spiritual writer, says: "Then, one perfect turning to God in the center of the heart is of more value than many other different exercises and works and is able to make up for lost opportunities of ten years or more.... The soul rejoices with a happy, peaceful liberty of mind, raised above cares, above all disturbances, above all fear of death, purgatory, hell and all things that can happen to it in time and in eternity." And again: "Those who are united with God in this way (directly) and allow Him to act freely in them, are the most dear friends of God, and in one little hour they are of more advantage to the Church than others who have not attained to this union can be in many years."

The reason is that they have been completely dead and crucified to all self-love in all its forms, so that Christ literally lives and acts freely in them in the use of their body and soul and in all the acts of their faculties and senses, continuing in them His redemptive life of prayer, work, and suffering. No wonder their apostolic work bears such rich harvests—they are produced by Christ living in their souls. What St. Paul said of himself, applies to them: "I live, now not I, but Christ lives in me."

"Taste and See That the Lord Is Sweet"

This delightful invitation, "taste and see," is extended to each of us. We are encouraged not merely to be satisfied with knowing by faith, but to know also by experience the joys which living with God in our hearts brings us. The difference between knowledge and experience can best be illustrated by some examples.

We may read all about the sweetness of honey, but tasting one drop of it tells us better what it is than a whole book about it.

On a dark night we may know well all the surroundings of our garden—the kind of trees, the variety and colors of the flowers, etc.—we know them. But how different is our knowledge of them when we see them in all their splendor on a bright sunny day.

We know the rose is contained in the swelling bud, but how different is our knowledge and joy when we see the bud opened and the rose in full bloom.

We see the caterpillar crawling slowly along the ground, not really a thing of beauty; perhaps later we see the cocoon or chrysalis, but when we see the butterfly which comes forth from it, what a difference!

The egg contains the chick, but what a difference when we see the chick itself.

So spiritually: "Taste and see that the Lord is sweet!" Experience it! Have courage! By persevering efforts in removing the obstacles we arrive at intimacy, at familiarity with God in our heart. True, St. Thérèse says: "It is not easy to become familiar with Jesus; one does not become so in a day." Persevering effort is all that is needed—God's grace does the rest.

A Final Exhortation

(Imitation of Christ, Bk. II, C. 1, v. 4ff.)

Christ will come to you and give you His consolation, if only you will prepare in your heart a worthy place for Him to abide.

He frequently visits an interior person, carries on pleasant conversations with him, gives His delightful consolations, much peace, and shows toward him an astounding, an amazing familiarity.

Wake up, faithful soul! Prepare your heart for this Sweet Guest, this most Sweet Spouse, so that He will gladly come and live with you.

Advice of Cardinal Mercier

Here is a secret of holiness and happiness. Every day, for at least five minutes, keep your imagination quiet, shut your eyes and ears to all things of sense, to all sounds of earth, so as to be able to withdraw into the sanctuary of your baptized soul, which is the temple of the Holy Spirit, speaking there to that Holy Spirit, saying these or similar words: "O Holy Spirit, soul of my soul, I adore You. Enlighten, guide, console and strengthen me. Tell me what I ought to do, and command me to do it. I promise to be submissive in everything You permit to happen to me: only show me what is Your will."

You will be happy.

Be Thou My Vision

Be Thou my vision, O Lord of my heart,
Naught be all else to me, save that Thou art,
Thou my best thought in the day and the night,
Waking or sleeping Thy presence my light.

Be Thou my Wisdom, be Thou my True Word,
I ever with Thee and Thou with me, Lord;
Thou my Great Father, and I Thy true son;
Thou in me dwelling, and I with Thee one.

Riches I need not, nor man's empty praise,
Thou mine inheritance through all my days;
Thou, and Thou only, the first in my heart,
High King of heaven, my Treasure Thou art.

High King of heaven, Thou heaven's bright sun,
Grant me its joys after Vict'ry is won,
Christ of my own heart whatever befall,
Still be my Vision, O Ruler of all.

Short Prayers to God in My Heart

O Most Blessed Trinity, I believe You are living within me, I hope in You, I love You.

O Most Blessed Trinity who dwells in my soul, make me love You more and more.

God the Father, remain in me always as You remain in Jesus.

O Holy Spirit, sweet Guest of my soul, remain with me and make me ever remain with You.

Holy Spirit, Come

Holy Spirit, Lord of light!
From Thy clear celestial height,
Thy pure, beaming radiance give;
Come, Thou Father of the poor!
Come, with treasures which endure!
Come, Thou light of all that live!
Thou of all consolers best,
Visiting the troubled breast,
Dost refreshing peace bestow;
Thou in toil art comfort sweet;
Pleasant coolness in the heat;
Solace in the midst of woe.
Light immortal! Light divine!
Visit Thou these hearts of Thine,
And our inmost being fill.
If Thou take Thy grace away,
Nothing pure in man will stay;
All his good is turned to ill.
Heal our wounds—our strength renew;
On our dryness pour Thy dew;
Wash the stains of guilt away;
Bend the stubborn heart and will;
Melt the frozen, warm the chill;
Guide the steps that go astray.
Thou, on those who evermore
Thee confess and Thee adore,
In Thy sevenfold gifts descend.
Give them comfort when they die;

Give them life with Thee on high;
Give them joys which never end. Amen.

God, Holy Spirit

God, Holy Spirit, I believe You are really and truly present in my heart. I trust in You blindly and without any limits. I love You and give myself to You entirely and forever.

Consecration to the Holy Spirit

O Holy Spirit, Divine Spirit of light and love, I consecrate to You my understanding, my heart and my will, my whole being for time and for eternity. May my understanding always be submissive to Your heavenly inspirations and to the teachings of the Catholic Church of which You are the infallible Guide.

May my heart always be inflamed with love of God and of my neighbor. May my will always be conformed to the divine will, and may my whole life be a perfect imitation of the life and virtues of our Lord and Savior, Jesus Christ. To Him and the Father with You be honor and glory forever. Amen.

Prayer of St. Augustine

Breathe in me, O Holy Spirit,
    That my thoughts may all be holy.
Act in me, O Holy Spirit,
    That my work, too, may be holy.
Draw my heart, O Holy Spirit,
    That I love but what is holy.

Strengthen me, O Holy Spirit,
    To defend all that is holy.
Guard me, then, O Holy Spirit,
    That I always may be holy. Amen.

Most Blessed Trinity of love
    For whom the heart of man was made,
To You be praise in timeless song
    And everlasting homage paid.

The Great Father
Father Faber

There's a wideness in God's Mercy
    like the wideness of the sea.
There's a kindness in His Justice
    which is more than clemency.
There's no place where earth's sorrows
    are more felt than up in heaven.
There's no place where earth's failings
    have such kindly judgment given.
For the love of God is broader
    than the measure of man's mind.
And the Heart of the Eternal
    is more wonderfully kind.
But we make His Love too narrow
    by false limits of our own.
And we magnify His strictness
    with a zeal He will not own.
If our love were but more simple
    we would take Him at His word.
And our lives would be all sunshine
    in the sweetness of the Lord.

O Holy Spirit

O Holy Spirit, so near to me, yet so little regarded, so solicitous, yet so forgotten, I thank You for all Your graces. I worship Your adorable authority over me. I cling to Your loving guidance. Add this one more favor to all: grant me the grace to think often of Your Presence in my heart. Amen.

God, Holy Spirit

God, Holy Spirit, teach me to live with You always present in my heart!

PRAYERS

by Rev. James Alberione, SSP, STD

Founder of the Pauline Family

Consecration to the Most Holy Trinity

O divine Trinity, Father, Son and Holy Spirit, present and active in the Church and in the depths of my soul, I adore You, I thank You, I love You! And through the hands of Mary most holy, my Mother, I offer, give, and consecrate myself entirely to You for life and for eternity.

To You, heavenly Father, I offer, give and consecrate myself as Your child.

To You, Jesus Master, I offer, give and consecrate myself as Your brother (sister) and disciple.

To You, Holy Spirit, I offer, give and consecrate myself as "a living temple" to be consecrated and sanctified.

O Mary, Mother of the Church and my Mother, teach me to live, through the liturgy and the sacraments, in ever more intimate union with the three divine Persons, so that my whole life may be a "glory be to the Father, to the Son and to the Holy Spirit." Amen.

Invocations to the Divine Master

Jesus Master, sanctify my mind and increase my faith.

Jesus, teaching in the Church, draw everyone to Your school.

Jesus Master, deliver me from error, from vain thoughts, and from eternal darkness.

O Jesus, Way between the Father and us, I offer You everything and look to You for everything.

O Jesus, Way of sanctity, make me Your faithful imitator.

O Jesus Way, render me perfect as the Father who is in heaven.

O Jesus Life, live in me, so that I may live in You.

O Jesus Life, do not permit me to separate myself from You.

O Jesus Life, grant that I may live eternally in the joy of Your love.

O Jesus Truth, may I be light for the world.

O Jesus Way, may I be an example and model for others.

O Jesus Life, may my presence bring grace and consolation everywhere.

Prayer to the Holy Spirit

O divine Holy Spirit, eternal Love of the Father and of the Son, I adore You, I thank You, I love You, and I ask You pardon for all the times I have grieved You in myself and in my neighbor.

Descend with many graces during the holy ordination of bishops and priests, during the consecration of men and women religious, during the reception of Confirmation by all the faithful; be light, sanctity and zeal.

To You, O Spirit of Truth, I consecrate my mind, imagination and memory; enlighten me. May I know Jesus Christ our Master and understand His Gospel and the teaching of Holy Church. Increase in me the gifts of wisdom, knowledge, understanding and right judgment.

To You, O sanctifying Spirit, I consecrate my will. Guide me in Your will, sustain me in the observance of the commandments, in the fulfillment of my duties. Grant me the gifts of courage and reverence.

To You, O life-giving Spirit, I consecrate my heart. Guard and increase the divine life in me. Grant me the gift of filial love. Amen.

Act of Submission to the Will of God

My God, I do not know what will happen to me today. I only know that nothing will happen to me that was not foreseen by You and directed to my greater good from all eternity. This is enough for me.

I adore Your holy, eternal and unfathomable designs. I submit to them with all my heart for love of You. I make a sacrifice of my whole being to You and join my sacrifice to that of Jesus, my divine Savior.

In His name and by His infinite merits, I ask You to give me patience in my sufferings and perfect submission, so that everything You want or permit to happen will result in Your greater glory and my sanctification. Amen.

Short Act of Consecration to Jesus Through Mary

I am all Yours and all that I possess I offer to You, my lovable Jesus, through Mary, Your most holy Mother.

Before Reading Sacred Scripture

O Jesus Christ, our Master, You are the Way and the Truth and the Life. Grant that we may learn the sublime wisdom of Your charity in the spirit of St. Paul the Apostle and of the Catholic Church. Send Your Holy Spirit to teach us and remind us of what You preached.

Jesus Master, Way and Truth and Life, have mercy on us.

After Reading Sacred Scripture

Jesus, Divine Master, You have words of eternal life.

I believe, O Lord and *Truth,* but increase my faith.

I love You, O Lord and *Way,* with all my strength, because You have commanded us to observe Your commandments perfectly.

I pray to You, O Lord and *Life:* I adore You, I praise You, I beseech You, and I thank You for the gift of the Sacred Scriptures.

With Mary, I shall remember and preserve Your words in my mind and I shall meditate on them in my heart.

Jesus Master, Way and Truth and Life, have mercy on us.

Those who devoutly read Sacred Scripture as spiritual reading gain a *partial indulgence.* If the reading lasts at least a half hour, the *indulgence* will be *plenary* (cf. *Manual of Indulgences,* no. 50).

Before Reading Correspondence and Receiving People

Jesus Master, enlighten my mind to understand well those who write or speak to me. Let me hear correctly; grant that I may answer in You and according to You. Dispose their hearts and my heart to seek only Your glory and the peace of hearts.

For Trips

O Jesus-Truth, enlighten me to travel only and always in charity and with my gaze fixed on heaven, my ultimate destination.

O Jesus-Way, be my guide, so that I may have complete self-control, a sure eye, and constant moderation.

O Jesus-Life, be for me everywhere, and for those whom I accompany or meet, joy of spirit and salvation of soul and body.

O my angel, kindly precede me and guard me. Amen.

Prayer Before Meals

Bless us, O Lord, and the food we are about to receive to keep us in Your holy service.

Prayer After Meals

We give You thanks for the food we have received, O Lord. Grant that it may always sustain us in Your holy service.

APPENDIX

Virtue

A *virtue* is a *power to do good* or a habit of doing good.

The main God-given virtues are the theological (God-centered) virtues and cardinal (hinge or key) virtues. Although these powers are free gifts of God, we must use them, so that they truly become the habits of doing good that God meant them to be.

Theological Virtues

Faith is the virtue by which we believe in God and everything He has taught us.

Hope is the virtue by which we trust that our all-powerful and faithful God will bring us to heaven if we live as He asks us to live.

Charity is the virtue by which we love God above everything else and love all other people for His sake.

Moral Virtues

Prudence is the virtue by which a person puts heaven before everything else, thinks carefully before acting, makes wise choices, and does things well.

Justice is the virtue by which a person is fair to everyone—first of all, to God.

Fortitude is the virtue by which a person does what is good and right in spite of any difficulty.

Temperance is the virtue by which a person exercises self-control with regard to the drives of human nature.

Gifts of the Holy Spirit

The gifts of the Holy Spirit are wisdom, understanding, right judgment (or counsel), courage (or fortitude), knowledge, reverent love (or piety) and holy fear.

Wisdom is the gift which helps us to love spiritual things, to put God in the first place in our lives, and to look at everything either as a help or an obstacle to reaching heaven.

The gift of *understanding* helps us to see more deeply into the truths we already believe by faith.

Right judgment helps us to choose what is right, even in difficult circumstances.

Courage is the gift which helps us to be brave and patient in overcoming difficulties and carrying out our duties.

Knowledge is the gift which helps us to know God and what He expects of us through what He has created.

Reverent love helps us to love God as our Father and all people as our brothers and sisters, so that we will serve both Him and them.

Holy fear helps us to respect God and to want to please Him in everything.

Fruits of the Holy Spirit

The fruits of the Holy Spirit are good deeds and habits that result from our response to the Holy Spirit's impulses to do good (actual graces). The gifts are: *charity, joy, peace, patience, kindness, goodness, long-suffering, humility, fidelity, modesty, continence, chastity.*

Humility is the virtue by which we truly know ourselves and see that whatever is good in us comes from God.

The Beatitudes

1. Blessed are the poor in spirit; for theirs is the kingdom of heaven.

2. Blessed are the meek; for they shall possess the land.

3. Blessed are they that mourn; for they shall be comforted.

4. Blessed are they that hunger and thirst after justice; for they shall have their fill.

5. Blessed are the merciful; for they shall obtain mercy.

6. Blessed are the clean of heart; for they shall see God.

7. Blessed are the peacemakers; for they shall be called the children of God.

8. Blessed are they that suffer persecution for justice' sake; for theirs is the kingdom of heaven.

Blessed are you when they shall revile you and persecute you and speak all that is evil against you, untruly, for my sake; be glad and rejoice, for your reward is very great in heaven; for so they persecuted the prophets that were before you (Mt. 5:3-12).

Daughters of St. Paul

MASSACHUSETTS
50 St. Paul's Ave., Jamaica Plain, Boston, MA 02130; **617-522-8911.**
172 Tremont Street, Boston, MA 02111; **617-426-5464; 617-426-4230.**
NEW YORK
78 Fort Place, Staten Island, NY 10301; **718-447-5071; 718-447-5086.**
59 East 43rd Street, New York, NY 10017; **212-986-7580.**
625 East 187th Street, Bronx, NY 10458; **212-584-0440.**
525 Main Street, Buffalo, NY 14203; **716-847-6044.**
NEW JERSEY
Hudson Mall—Route 440 and Communipaw Ave.,
Jersey City, NJ 07304; **201-433-7740.**
CONNECTICUT
202 Fairfield Ave., Bridgeport, CT 06604; **203-335-9913.**
OHIO
2105 Ontario Street (at Prospect Ave.), Cleveland, OH 44115;
216-621-9427.
616 Walnut Street, Cincinnati, OH 45202; **513-421-5733; 513-721-5059.**
PENNSYLVANIA
1719 Chestnut Street, Philadelphia, PA 19103; **215-568-2638.**
VIRGINIA
1025 King Street, Alexandria, VA 22314; **703-683-1741; 703-549-3806.**
SOUTH CAROLINA
243 King Street, Charleston, SC 29401; **803-577-0175.**
FLORIDA
2700 Biscayne Blvd., Miami, FL 33137; **305-573-1618; 305-573-1624.**
LOUISIANA
4403 Veterans Memorial Blvd., Metairie, LA 70006; **504-887-7631;
504-887-0113.**
423 Main Street, Baton Rouge, LA 70802; **504-343-4057; 504-381-9485.**
MISSOURI
1001 Pine Street (at North 10th), St. Louis, MO 63101; **314-621-0346;
314-231-1034.**
ILLINOIS
172 North Michigan Ave., Chicago, IL 60601; **312-346-4228; 312-346-3240.**
TEXAS
114 Main Plaza, San Antonio, TX 78205; **512-224-8101; 512-224-0938.**
CALIFORNIA
1570 Fifth Ave. (at Cedar St.), San Diego, CA 92101; **619-232-1442.**
46 Geary Street, San Francisco, CA 94108; **415-781-5180.**
WASHINGTON
2301 Second Ave., Seattle, WA 98121; **206-441-3300.**
HAWAII
1143 Bishop Street, Honolulu, HI 96813; **808-521-2731.**
ALASKA
750 West 5th Ave., Anchorage, AK 99501; **907-272-8183.**

CANADA
3022 Dufferin Street, Toronto 395, Ontario, Canada.